DEATH CARE

THE HEALTH COVERAGE YOU NEED AFTER YOU DIE

DEATH CARE

JAMIE BATTIEST

Death Care
Copyright © 2020 by Jamie Battiest. All rights reserved.

No part of this publication may be reproduced, stored in a retrieval system or transmitted in any way by any means, electronic, mechanical, photocopy, recording or otherwise without the prior permission of the author except as provided by USA copyright law.

The opinions expressed by the author are not necessarily those of URLink Print and Media.

1603 Capitol Ave., Suite 310 Cheyenne, Wyoming USA 82001
1-888-980-6523 | admin@urlinkpublishing.com

URLink Print and Media is committed to excellence in the publishing industry.

Book design copyright © 2020 by URLink Print and Media. All rights reserved.

Published in the United States of America
ISBN 978-1-64753-375-5 (Paperback)
ISBN 978-1-64753-376-2 (Digital)

13.05.20

DEDICATION

I dedicate this book to my family and friends. I love you all and pray that you all may know the Lord, Jesus Christ, as your Savior.

CONTENTS

Dedication..................................5
Introduction 9
Investigation of Death Cases....................11
Jerry....................................17
Stan....................................23
Jason...................................33
Tyler 43
Christine................................53
Kaitlyn..................................61
While We're Alive..........................71
Questions 77
You, Me, and Grandma......................87
Death...................................91
Bibliography 93
Endnotes................................95

INTRODUCTION

I have been asked what it was that caused me to write this book. It was the conversation I had with a good friend that sparked the fire for this book. I had spoken to this friend several times about things of eternity, but she, like so many other people I know and love, has the view that there's plenty of time to worry about eternity later. I talked with my husband about this attitude that so many people have, and we discussed the sad reality of how many people we knew who died sudden deaths. There was no "later" for them. We all know that millions of people die every day, yet we change to also assume it won't be us. I thought that perhaps a book with several true-to-life stories would perhaps cause the reader to stop and think about the fact that they have no promise of tomorrow. I wanted them to ask, "After death, then what?" And I wanted to provide some good answers. The conversation with my friend is included in one of the chapters of this book. Each story is of a real person whom my husband or I knew. The circumstances of their deaths are very real and not fictional. Some of the events that I include leading up to their deaths are fictional, to a degree, because there isn't any realistic way for me to know exactly what was said and done before their deaths, but please keep in mind that most of it is very true. May it cause us all to stop, think, and reflect about our life here on earth and what our eternity will be.

INVESTIGATION OF DEATH CASES

Congress is preparing to begin an investigation into the billion-dollar health care industry. Accusations of misappropriation of funds and the total lack of accountability on the part of the health care industry to properly address the cases of death that have continually plagued our nation for generations have been launched. In spite of pouring billions of dollars annually into the health care system, fatalities from death remain at 100 percent. The President is preparing to call a state of emergency if this growing epidemic continues.

The numerous medical organizations, including the American Medical Association, have already begun protesting the investigation. The CEO of the AMA, Dr. Joseph Pendyke, released this statement:

> We are doing all that we can to find a cure for this terminal epidemic. Our

doctors and nurses are doing their very best to treat every case that comes in. You cannot possibly hold them accountable for something that is completely beyond their control. We are hoping that we will soon have a vaccination to help prevent the spread of death but so far we have been unable to isolate the cause and therefore all of our inoculations thus far have been ineffective. However, given more time and more funds we are certain that we can find a cure.

In the midst of this death scandal, a group of concerned citizens are taking action and speaking out against the medical establishment. The spokesperson for this group is Ms. Ima Living. We contacted her, and she had this to say:

It is time that we the people stand up to the health care industry, the funeral industry, and the government and demand that we see some results in the fight against this scourge of death. We pay billions of dollars into the system, and what do we get for our money? Nothing. Zero. Zip. Zilch. Nada. Why should we continue to spend our hard- earned money to prevent death only to end up dying anyway? One hundred percent of people who contract death experience a permanent cessation of all vital functions, resulting in the end of life. Someone needs to be held accountable for the fraud passed off as "modern medicine," which has been deceiving and using the American people for years. We believe that the health care industry, the funeral industry, and the government are right in cahoots. We are tired of this, and we want to see results *now*.

Congressional hearings are slated to begin in three weeks. Will the health care industry be able to vindicate themselves, or will heads begin to roll? Already, there is talk of the President removing the current CEO of the AMA. However, in light of the current hearings and possible ramifications, finding a qualified person to accept the position might prove to be very difficult.

Okay. So maybe that article is a bit obtuse. But have you ever wondered why we call it *health care*? Would not *death care* be a more appropriate name? After all, isn't that what we are all trying to avoid? We pay millions of dollars every year to hospitals, doctors' offices, and emergency care clinics. We go for preventative care, and when anything significant, like a cough or cold, occurs we go again. We can feel perfectly fine, yet we go and pay for "preventative" tests and "screenings." No one wants to be sick, but what we really are trying to prevent is death.

Some people spend money on health food, fitness and workout equipment, gym fees, weight loss pills, and fad diets. Why? They want to lose weight and keep fit. Why would they want to do that? As one pessimistic person so succinctly put it, "Eat right, keep fit, die anyway." That is just the plain honest truth. It is a sad fact that ten out of every ten people die.

Death and death-related businesses make millions of dollars every year. Not just the health care end of it, but think of the insurance side. You pay money to have "life" insurance, but you do not receive any return on that investment until you are dead. Even then, *you* are not the *beneficiary*.

Then, when you die, there is the funeral home and burial expenses to be paid. Some people save money by going with cremation, yet it still isn't cheap. We spend money to stay alive but die anyway, in addition it costs more money to die. However, despite all of our "prevention" measures, one day we all will die.

I am only thirty-one years old as of this writing. Through my short lifetime, I have attended a good number of funerals for different friends and family. I know what it is like to get the awful phone call with the news of a loved one dying. I know what it is to stand over the coffin of a person who was cut off in the middle of a beautiful life. I have cried and felt the sorrow of death. Then one day, it dawned on me. *That could be me.* Here I am, driving past the funeral home, feeling the sorrow of loss, but thankfully, *I am still alive.*

So that led me to ask, "Why? Why am I lucky enough to still be alive?" In 2006, over eighty thousand young people died before they reached the age of thirty[1]. I could have been one of those who died, but I wasn't. Every thirty-one minutes, someone dies in a drunk driving accident[2]. I even had a coworker who came close to dying in such an accident, yet I am alive and healthy. Why? What is so special about me?

That was when I realized that there is nothing special about me. Death is waiting for me, too. I just do not know when or where. It could happen today or maybe tomorrow. Death might not come for another decade or two. There is no way for me to know for certain. And when I die, then what? What if death is not the end but merely the beginning of eternity?

The following chapters are a collection of true stories of people who met death very suddenly and unexpectedly. Some are fairly common deaths, and some are more of what you call "freak" accidents, but bear in mind that they are true. Death was the last thing these people were expecting. Yet it came to these healthy, happy individuals who were simply living their lives just like you right now.

JERRY

Jerry blinked and tried not to fall asleep. He had been up since 4:00 a.m., and it was now going on 10:00 a.m. He had been sitting in his deer stand, waiting for that big buck that he knew lived in that part of the woods. Patience was the name of the game when you were deer hunting, but Jerry was almost ready to call it a day. He let his mind wander from deer hunting to thoughts of his family. His oldest daughter would be having his second grandchild in a few weeks. Jerry could hardly wait. Grandchildren are the reward for not killing your own children when they were little. And they are twice as much fun.

Jerry's thoughts jerked his attention back to the field before him. Something was stirring just behind the berry thicket, which was directly behind him. He almost held his breath as the big twelve-point buck walked right out from under his tree. He waited as the buck cautiously edged out toward the little creek that ran through the field. The buck drank slowly from the stream and turned so that he was standing broadside to Jerry. Jerry raised his rifle slowly.

The buck twitched his ears and turned his head in Jerry's direction, ready to leap at the first sense of danger. It was too late. Jerry already had him in his sights, and with one squeeze of the trigger, he brought the beautiful buck down.

After field dressing his buck, Jerry took it to the ranger station to check it in and weigh it. Then he took it by his friend Lonnie Burton's to have it butchered. Jerry loved to eat venison almost as much as he loved hunting. Jerry would cook it himself because, in addition to being a good hunter, he was also a good cook. His wife certainly appreciated his culinary skills too.

Ah, his wife. Jerry and Susan had been married for thirty-five years. They had three great kids and one and a half grandkids. Jerry laughed as he thought about his first grandchild, Jackson. The boy had a nature similar to his granddad. He even favored Jerry a bit in his looks. Yes, Jackson was Jerry's lil buddy. Jerry took him to the park and to his favorite fishing spot. They had lots of fun together. Soon, Jackson would have a little sister to include in the fun.

Jackson wasn't too sure about having a sister, however. He was only four and thought that girls were "ick." He had specifically asked for a brother and just couldn't understand why his parents were giving him a sister instead. When they first found out the baby was a girl, he had looked up at his mom, Vicki, and asked, "Well, after you have this sister, *then* can you have my baby brother?"

The answer to that was a definite no. In fact, Vicki was scheduled to have surgery while she was in postpartum recovery to ensure that there would be no more siblings for

Jackson. Jackson didn't know about any of that, nor did he need to. He would learn about all of that in due time.

Jerry's cell phone rang and brought him back to the present. It was Susan. He had made plans to take her to lunch but was running late. "I'm on my way, dear. I should be there in twenty minutes."

Susan never nagged him about anything. She was a very patient lady. It made Jerry smile just thinking about her. He loved doing things for her. He was her king, and she was his queen. It had always been that way for thirty-five years.

Jerry had also worked at the same company for thirty-five years. He had been able to invest his money wisely and, combined with the retirement that came from the company, was able to retire very comfortably at the age of fifty-seven. Life was perfect.

He'd only been retired for a few months when he began having pain in his lower back. The pain would radiate from his back to his groin area. It was excruciating. He hated going to the doctor but was forced to make a trip to the ER one night when the pain became more than he could bear. The diagnosis was kidney stones.

The ER doctor recommended that Jerry go see his personal physician the next day to determine what sort of treatment should be done. Jerry did, and his doctor decided that lithotripsy would be the best way to get rid of the kidney stones.

Dr. Duncan explained to Jerry, "In this procedure, lithotripsy, we bombard the kidney stones with ultrasonic radiation to make them smaller and easier to pass. It's a fairly simple procedure that usually presents no problems, but I think I want to hospitalize you for probably twenty-four hours so that we can monitor you and make sure that the stones are passing."

"That sounds fine to me, Doc," Jerry said. "Let's do it. I'm ready to be through with this."

So Jerry was admitted to the hospital, and the lithotripsy procedure was done. The nurses monitored him to ensure that it had worked and the stones were starting to pass. It was late that evening when Jerry received a phone call from his son-in-law.

"Please send Susan to the birthing center. Vicki's in labor!"

"What? Are you here in the hospital right now?" Jerry winced as he sat up and looked over at his wife, who was on the edge of her seat.

"Yes, we are in the birth center. Vicki is dilated to a five, and her water has broken. Things are moving pretty quickly, so please send Susan down," came the reply.

Jerry hung up the phone and turned to Susan. "Well, looks like the whole family is going to be here before the night is up. Vicki's in labor, and she wants you to go to the birthing center."

Susan was torn for just a second. "But what about you, Dear?"

Jerry laughed. "I'll be fine. I just wish I could be down there too! Go on. Don't forget ol' Granddad. Be sure to come and tell me as soon as the baby's born. Now get going!"

Susan was out the door and down the hall in a flash. Jerry sank back into his pillow, smiling. He would have to go and see his little granddaughter before he checked out of the hospital. Hopefully, that would be tomorrow morning, early.

Dr. Duncan came in the next morning before 9:00 a.m. "The procedure seems to have worked. Everything looks good. You can leave just after lunch today. We just want to watch you for a few more hours to make sure that everything is copacetic, and then you can go home."

Jerry grinned at the doctor. "Thank you, but I'm not leaving immediately. I have to stop by the newborn nursery. My granddaughter was born last night, and I intend to hold her before I leave the hospital!"

Dr. Duncan looked up from his chart. "Well, congratulations, Jerry. I'll check back in on you just after lunch and sign your release papers. Have a nice day."

Jerry nodded, and the doctor left.

Just after lunch, the doctor came in and spoke briefly with Jerry. The nurse followed the doctor, giving instructions to Jerry for his recovery at home. She gave him his release papers and told him he could get his clothes on and leave any time. While the nurse was giving Jerry his instructions, Jerry's friend, Tim, came in.

"Hey, looks like you're ready to leave! I was coming by to visit with you, but I guess I'll just have to stop by your house in a little while instead." Tim slapped Jerry on the back.

Jerry was sitting up on the edge of the bed, preparing to get up and get his clothes on.

"Yep, but I'm going to see Vicki first. Did you hear?"

Tim cut Jerry off. "I ran into Susan on my way up here. She told me about the grandbaby. Congrats, Jerry!"

"Thanks. Now get outta here so I can get my clothes on and go see her." Jerry waved Tim out of the room.

Tim replied, "Okay, but how 'bout if I wait here in the hall and walk down with you? I would like to congratulate Vicki and see the baby myself."

Jerry nodded. "Sure. I'll only take a minute."

Tim stepped out and had barely shut the door when he heard a loud *thud*. He knocked on the door, but there was no response. He cracked the door and said, "Hey, Jerry, what's going on in there?"

Still no response.

Tim slowly opened the door, and what he saw brought panic. "Nurse! Help! Come quick!"

Jerry had collapsed in a heap on the floor.

Two nurses came in. "Code Blue! Code Blue!"

Tim stepped back as nurses and aides swarmed the room. A doctor appeared from somewhere, and Jerry was wheeled out of his room to the ICU. They tried to revive him, but it was no use. A clot had reached his brain, and death had come.

Just like that, Jerry was gone. He never got to see his infant granddaughter. He was no kid, he knew that death was a very real thing but it was the last thing he expected on that day. Was he ready to face what eternity held for him? He needed Death Care.

STAN

Stan and Son Brick Masonry. Well, that's what it had been until his son decided it was time to branch out on his own. His son, Reid, had been hired at the new retail lumber store a few months back. Stan smiled as he thought of his son. They'd worked together for almost six years. In that time, they had grown as close as a father and son could. Now his son was working at his own job and had even gotten married. He shook his head. Kids grow up, and you have to let them go.

Stan enjoyed laying brick, but it was most often feast or famine. Either he was swamped with work or he had no work. That's how it is in construction when you're an independent worker. Before he became a brick mason, he'd worked in the oil field some and had driven a truck some. It had paid much better, or at least more consistently, but he didn't like the long hours and being away from his family so much. In life, you have to make choices. He had chosen a job that allowed for more time with his family, sometimes more time at home than at work. It could be rough, and it had often been very tight financially, but they always managed to get by. That was just life. Everyone's life leads down a different road. He'd had his share of difficulties in his fifty-four-year life span, but he'd also had plenty of blessings, the biggest of those being his family.

In addition to his son and daughter-in-law, he had his wife of thirty years, Lynn; his daughter, Michelle; and his granddaughter, Emma. Who knows? With his son newly married, maybe his family would be growing again soon. He smiled. Maybe he would soon have another granddaughter or even a grandson. Yes, he was blessed in so many ways. So what if things were rough occasionally? It made the good times all the more sweet.

Stan felt a tug on his sleeve.

"Pawpaw. Juice."

He looked down at this two-year-old granddaughter, Emma. "I don't have any juice, but how'd you like a drink of Pawpaw's tea?"

Stan shared his drink with Emma. He shared everything with Emma. Some people would say that he spoiled her, but that's what grandparents are for, right?

Her mom, Michelle, was a single mom. She had come back home to live with Stan and Lynn when she found out that she was expecting Emma. Emma's dad had never taken responsibility for Emma. He had signed away his rights to even see the child. So Stan and Lynn had stepped in to help Michelle raise Emma. They all pulled together as a family to take care of Emma—well, really, to take care of each other.

When Stan and Emma had finished both his glass of tea and the sandwich he had made, it was time to put Emma down for her nap. He pulled out his guitar to play and sing to her. Stan was a very good guitar player as well as an excellent singer. His dad had also been a singer. He was a bass singer, to be exact. Stan was not a bass singer, but he had a nice vocal range, and nothing soothed Emma to sleep so quickly or easily as her Pawpaw's singing.

Emma curled up on the sofa as Stan began to play an old folk song, "Jimmy Brown the Newspaper Boy."

"I sell the morning paper, sir. My name is Jimmy Brown. Everybody knows that I'm the newsboy of this town…"

Stan liked the old country and folk songs but especially gospel songs. He sang a combination of all three, and soon, he looked over to find Emma sound asleep. Stan smiled and set his guitar on its stand. He picked Emma up and took her to her toddler bed. There's nothing as precious as a little one sleeping. Stan looked at Emma for a long moment before turning out her light. *They grow so fast.* It seemed like only a few years ago, he was putting her mama, Michelle, to bed in the same way.

Stan shook his head and went back to his guitar. Soon, his wife and daughter would be home. It would be nice to have dinner as a family at the dining table tonight. They most often ate in shifts. One would come in and fix something, and about the time they were headed out the door to work, the other would be coming in. Such was their life.

The household flowed from day to day with Stan, Lynn, and Michelle all going to work at different times, all of them pulling together to take care of Emma. One Sunday evening, Stan decided to take his son and new daughter-in- law out to eat. There was a nice hometown burger joint not far from their house. It was what some might call a "greasy spoon." But the food was homemade and fresh. You just couldn't beat it.

"Well, son, how do you like your new job?" Stan asked after they were seated.

Reid replied, "Oh, I like it fine. I really enjoyed seeing you come in the other day, Dad. It sure was cute." He turned to his wife, Sandra, and mother. "I was squatting down stocking boxes of nails when I felt this little hand on my back and head. 'Unka Reid.' I turned around and saw Emma! What a surprise. I loved it."

Everyone smiled at that.

"How is your work going, Dad? Do you have some jobs lined out for the summer?" Reid asked.

"Oh yeah. I've got some work I'm about to start," was Stan's reply.

Their food was delivered, interrupting the conversation.

Little did his son know that things were pretty tight at home. He really needed a helper. The work went so much faster when he wasn't working alone. Quick work pleased the customer and also allowed room for more jobs, which meant more money. But he would never voice those thoughts to his son. He didn't want Reid to feel any guilt for leaving him on his own. He couldn't hire another helper quite like Reid and really couldn't afford to pay one right now either. But he wouldn't burden his son with those things. Reid had a new wife to worry about caring for and making a life with. Things would work out. They always did.

Sometime a few weeks later, Stan decided he would take Michelle out to lunch. He had finally finished a couple of jobs and caught his bills up, so he had a little cash to spend. They had not been, just the two of them, in a long time. Well, it really wouldn't be just the two of them. They'd have Emma too. That girl is so feisty! You cannot get her to stay in her carseat. She's a little Houdini. Stan or Michelle would strap her into the seat, but almost before they were out of the drive, she would be out bouncing all over the car. What is a body to do with a young'un like that? Stan chuckled to himself. All he knew was to just love her, and that was easy to do.

Michelle, Emma, and Stan went to their favorite Mexican restaurant for lunch together. It was nice to slow down and have a relaxed conversation. Michelle worked for a local retirement center. Stan's mother lived in the retirement center, so Michelle tried to keep an eye on her as much as possible.

Michelle kept Stan updated on his mother. "Grandma has been doing pretty good lately. Sometimes they forget that she takes Sweet'N Low with her tea. They keep trying to give her Splenda instead. That frustrates her."

"Yes, she has to have her Sweet 'N' Low. I'm glad to hear she is doing all right. Does Walter get down to see her often?" Stan inquired.

Walter was Stan's stepfather.

"He's there every day, Dad. I'm glad that he comes to visit, but, honestly, the man gets on my nerves. I wonder why he doesn't move into the center with Grandma. It doesn't make sense for him to hang onto that house when he's the only one living there." Michelle continued to voice her opinion of her grandparents' living situation as Stan listened.

After a while, Stan asked, "How are you and Greg doing?"

Greg was Michelle's boyfriend. They'd been dating for a little over a year now.

Michelle smiled and bobbed her head. "Good. We're good. He's really fond of little Emma. She likes him too. We have a date tomorrow night, just me and Greg. Mom said she'd watch Emma for us."

Stan agreed, "Yeah, we can handle her for you while you and Greg are out. Just remember the curfew." He said this with a look, and Michelle knew he was teasing. She laughed. "I'm twenty-nine! Remind me again what my curfew is?"

They laughed together, but Stan had to act fast to catch Emma's sippy cup before it hit the floor.

"Whew! Quick reflexes, Dad. At least you intercepted one mess before it happened." Michelle smiled across at her Dad before turning her attention to Emma.

"Emma, you need to eat. What do you want to eat?"

Emma replied in her sweet little voice, "Meat. I want meat."

So they ate and talked. It was a very nice evening.

A day or two later, Stan was out working in the hot sun, bricking a patio. The backyard he was working in was fairly shaded but the weather was still pretty hot for a man of his age to endure for very long. He mopped the sweat away with his handkerchief and reached for his tea jug.

Whew! It must be at least a hundred degrees, Stan thought.

He would really love to stop and go home early. It was the heat of the day and very difficult to make his body keep going. But Stan didn't feel like he could stop just yet. He was supposed to start another job next week and really needed to finish this one first. He only lacked about two days of work on it if he could put in a full work day. He also needed to collect the payment for this patio. He'd had to take his guitar to the pawn shop the other day to get some extra cash to pay for a new tire on his work truck. It was just that way sometimes. Bills came due or vehicles needed repairs. Cash ran low, and he just couldn't seem to work as fast as he used to.

Stan worked a while longer and reached a place where he felt he had to stop. Well, he'd not gotten as far as he'd hoped, but he simply could not keep going. Something seemed wrong, but he couldn't put his finger on it. He didn't feel well.

Stan shook his head and thought, *It's not fun getting old. Your body just starts to fail you.* But he smiled as he loaded up some of his tools. *Time to go home and eat supper.*

He knew that Lynn would have supper ready. She would certainly have a nice glass of ice-cold tea waiting for him when he got home. Stan set his big tea jug into his truck for the ride home. He wasn't feeling so great, but if he could just get home, relax under the air conditioner a while and get a nice shower, things would be fine. There was a time when working out in the heat wouldn't have bothered him so much. "But," he thought, "I'm no spring chicken anymore." No, and when he was younger he hadn't had diabetes to deal with, either. His body tired more easily than it used to. Things were just as he expected when he reached home. Greg was there with Michelle, and they were preparing to take Emma to the park for a while. He said good-bye to them before getting cleaned up and sitting down to eat. He was mulling over whether or not he should go to church. It was Wednesday, and he wasn't quite sure if he felt up to attending the midweek church service at their small church. He still wasn't feeling quite right.

Stan finally decided he would go. "Are you ready for church, Lynn?" Stan got up from the table and went to get his shoes.

Lynn came out of their bedroom and said, "I'm ready if you're sure you feel up to going."

Stan shook his head but said, "I'll be all right. I'll talk to Reid about how I'm feeling, and we'll have everyone pray. But I think I'd better let you drive."

So Lynn climbed in behind the steering wheel of Stan's truck, and off they went. Once they reached the highway, they would drive seven miles north to the church. However, by the time they had driven the three miles to the highway, Stan changed his mind. His chest had felt strange all afternoon. He'd passed it off as heartburn at first, or perhaps his blood sugar being a bit high. But now there was quite a bit of pain. It began to get worse and was starting to take his breath away.

He told Lynn, "No…go to the hospital…Get me…to the hospital."

Lynn began to feel panicked. She looked at Stan's face.

Oh no! Not a heart attack!

He'd never had heart trouble before, not even high blood pressure.

Please not a heart attack!

Stan looked out of his window at the passing landscape. How many times had he driven past that same scenery? Too many times to even count. He could close his eyes and still see it all. Then his eyes did close, tightly, with the increasing pain in his chest. When he opened them next, he saw things in a haze. Stan closed his eyes one last time, and his body slumped in the passenger seat.

Lynn frantically began to shake his shoulder and call, "Stan! Stan! Please wake up! Stan!"

But Stan did not wake up. Death came, and Stan left. All was done.

Most of us believe that we will have little clues before a heart attack hits. We seem to think there will always be time, always a second chance. That is not the case. Death quite often comes very suddenly, unexpectedly. Stan had never had heart trouble before. But he had looked at death long ago and asked the questions about what eternity might hold for him. He had sought for Death Care and found the answer. His eternity was covered.

JASON

Jason McCaskill walked into his parents' house and flipped on the light in the family room.

"Surprise! Happy birthday, Jason!"

He was shocked to see all of his teammates from his swim team standing in the front room. The whole house was decked out for his eighteenth birthday.

Jason grinned. "Thanks for the party. Now, where's the cake?"

Everyone laughed at that.

His best friend, Nick, piped up, "It'll be pretty hard to play a good game of volleyball with a stomach full of cake!"

Taylor chimed in, "Yeah. We have the net already set up out back. Come on. Let's go play a game while your dad grills the burgers."

"Great! Let's hit it!"

They played volleyball until it was dark. Then they ate their burgers and cut cake. Of course, after the cake came the gifts. Jason knew his parents had been scheming about some big surprise for his birthday, but he thought the party was it. Boy, was he wrong.

"What's this?" Jason asked as his dad, Scott McCaskill, handed him a large box and an envelope.

"Open the envelope first, son." His dad was grinning from ear to ear, but Sara, his mom, had sort of an anxious look on her face as Jason ripped into the envelope. After a pause, Nick said, "Well, what is it, Jason? We're all waiting to hear!"

"A certificate." Jason was quiet as he read the certificate.

"What kind of certificate?" Randy quizzed.

"It's for a repelling lesson, right, Dad?" Jason finally said.

Randy cut his eyes at Jason, "What? Spelling lessons?"

Jason playfully punched Randy in the arm. "No, not *spelling*. *Repelling*, dork."

Jason's dad nodded. "And this is the equipment that you'll need." He indicated the box on the table.

Jason opened the box, and, sure enough, inside was all of the equipment he would need for repelling.

"You just call the number on that certificate and set up a time with the instructor. You could start this weekend if you wanted."

"Wow!" Jason said. "This rocks! Thanks, Dad! Thank you, Mom."

Jason hugged his mom, who smiled and said, "We know how much you enjoy the outdoors, son. Just pay attention to the instructor and be careful. All right?"

Jason wasn't really listening at that point. He and his friends were going through the equipment and talking about going repelling together. Nick and Randy had been repelling before on a camping trip. So they were experienced and knew exactly what to do. The three were already making plans to go repelling the next weekend, just as soon as Jason had had his "lessons" from the paid "instructor." It was just like parents to go and pay for an instructor when really all that was needed was the equipment and someone who had already been repelling to teach you. There wasn't much to it. Besides, Jason was eighteen. He was an adult. He could do whatever he wanted. But he would go take the lessons just because his parents wanted him to. He'd always been that kind of guy.

Jason knew that pretty soon, his relationship with his parents was going to change. He wasn't sure how much, but he knew that they would have to accept his independence and let him be an adult. After all, he was going to start college that fall. He had received an academic scholarship at a college several states away. He would be living on campus, away from his parents for the first time in his life, and that would definitely make things different. Jason smiled to himself. Finally, he would be on his own. It would be harder on his parents than it would be on him. He relished the thought of his independence. It was going to be great.

The following week, Jason called and arranged for his repelling "lesson." It was only a half-day class, and then they headed out to the mountains for supervised practice. Jason breezed through it. He was a natural at anything athletic. He was intelligent too.

And, he thought to himself with a grin, *I'm good looking to boot.*

Jason loved repelling. All through the summer, he spent most of his spare time at the mountains, repelling the different cliffs. He took Nick, Randy, or one of his other friends with him, and they had a blast. By the time he was ready to leave for his first semester of college, he was bronze from spending so much time on those rock cliffs.

Jason found his first year of college a pretty easy adjustment and was able to whiz through most of his classes and loved his newfound freedom. He had made several new friends, including a girl named Julie. Julie was beautiful, truly beautiful. She had long, curly, red hair and sparkling green eyes. She was also very witty and smart. Unfortunately, they did not have any classes together but saw one another frequently through their mutual friends. By the end of the school year, Jason and Julie had become an item. It was only natural for Jason to bring her home to meet his folks. Boy, were they surprised.

"Mom, Dad, this is Julie."

They had barely climbed out of the car before Jason was making introductions. It was easy to see that he was pretty nervous. But his mom and dad were cool. Gracious; if anyone fit that description, it was his mom, Sara McCaskill.

"It is so nice to meet you, Julie. Jason has mentioned you to us several times, but he forgot to tell us that he would be bringing you home to meet us." Sara smiled as she looked into Julie's eyes. It has been said that the eyes are the window of the soul, and she liked what she saw in Julie's eyes. She showed Julie into the front room while the men gathered luggage. "We had planned to take Jason out for supper tonight. We would still like to do that, to take both of you. That is, unless the two of you have made other plans."

Julie shook her head. "No. We really had not thought much beyond coming to see you guys. Whatever you had planned is fine for us, if you don't mind having an extra person along."

"Of course not! It will be nice to get to visit with you." Sara turned to direct her men as they came in through the door. "Jason, your room is ready, and Julie can take the guestroom, or did you plan for Julie to stay at a hotel?"

Jason looked from Julie to his mom, "Nah. No need for all that fuss. She and I can both stay in my room."

The air went a bit tense, and Jason saw his parents exchange a glance.

Then his dad spoke. "No, son, I'm afraid that arrangement would be uncomfortable for all of us. No. Julie is more than welcome to the guest room, but if the two of you feel you have to share a room, then I think you should go to the hotel. You know how we feel about that sort of thing. We understand that you are an adult and we cannot tell you how to live your life. However, when you are at home, we would like for you to respect our sentiments and house rules while you are here."

Jason couldn't do anything but shrug. At least his dad didn't lose it like Nick's dad had when Nick brought his girl, China, home and they wanted to share a room. Jason looked at his dad and then glanced at Julie. "Okay. Come on, Julie. Follow me to the guest room." With that, Jason led Julie down the hall, leaving his parents to simply stare after them.

They had dinner, and then his parents went back to the house. Jason and Julie decided to go to a late movie before coming back to his parents'. They got in bed late and slept in late the next morning. It was almost lunchtime before Sara heard them stir. She glanced down the hall when she heard Jason come out of his room.

He came into the kitchen and asked, "Hey, Mom. What have ya got for breakfast?" He opened the fridge and took out a coke.

"Well, Jason, I made bacon and eggs for your dad and myself. You are welcome to the same. I can cook it up for you in a few minutes." Sara went to the laundry room to load the washing machine. She heard Julie come out of the guest room and join Jason in the kitchen. By the time she made it into the kitchen, the two were seated at the breakfast nook, eating the chocolate cake she had just frosted and put aside for supper.

"What on earth?" She looked at Jason with her hands on her hips. "Boy, what do you think you are doing?"

Jason grinned sheepishly. "Well, you know I've not had your chocolate cake in a long time."

Sara had walked over to the table and was trying hard to look upset. But it wasn't easy. It reminded her so much of Jason as a young teenager, when his friends would sleep over and eat everything in sight.

My, time flies and kids grow up. Well, sort of, she thought as she watched her son.

"Okay. Enjoy it, Jason."

Jason grinned around another forkful of cake and winked at Julie.

Sara took a seat across from Jason. "Good morning, Julie. Do the two of you have plans for today?"

Jason nodded, but his mouth was full of the last bite of his cake.

Julie replied, "Jason is taking me to the mountains and showing me how much fun repelling can be."

The tone of her voice indicated to Sara that Julie was new to repelling.

She asked Julie, "Have you been around the mountains or seen others repel before?"

"No. I grew up in the city, and though I enjoy sports and stuff, I have never been, like, to the mountains or hiking or anything. But I'm sure it will be an interesting experience." She flashed a look at Jason, and he laughed.

"Jason, are you planning to take anyone else with you? I think Randy is home from school too. You should call him up and see if he would want to go with you."

But Jason shook his head at that. "Nah. I'll catch up with Randy later. Today, it's just me and Julie. We should be home by suppertime though." Jason stood to leave the table but turned to look at his mom again. "What time is supper tonight?"

"Your father gets off at five. Can you be home around then?"

Jason was halfway down the hall. "I think so."

It didn't take long for Julie and Jason to get out the door and head to the mountains. Sara watched them drive away from her family room window. *My, my how things* change. People change. *One day, Jason will be married. How much different will things be then?* Sara turned away and shook her head to clear her thoughts. It was getting late, and she was scheduled to volunteer at the hospital in thirty minutes. *Better get a move on. There will be plenty of time to think up worries later.*

Jason and Julie made it to the mountains where they hiked up to the shorter cliffs and repelled for an hour or two.

"What a great rush! But I am starved. I need a snack break." Julie was already digging through their pack. She pulled out some trail mix and granola bars.

As they sat eating their snack, Jason asked, "Well, how brave are you feeling? Are you up for a challenge?" He cut his eyes at Julie. Jason knew that Julie could not resist a challenge or a dare.

She looked him square in the eyes, "Bring it on!"

"Ok, let's hike on over there to the hundred-and-twenty- foot hole and repel there for a while."

Julie's eyes widened for a moment, and then she grinned. *What could go wrong?* "Sure. I'm game."

They reached the 120 foot hole, which was completely deserted on that day. Jason dropped their gear, and Julie's phone buzzed. She sat down to check out who was texting her while Jason began looking for a place to tie off.

"Ugh. My mom. She's hassling me about being out here, repelling. She is such a city slicker!"

Jason smiled. "So are you! You just happen to be one who likes to defy death."

Julie shot him a look but was too busy texting her mom for a comeback. Jason still had not spotted what he was looking for when he felt his foot slip, and his heart jumped into his throat. Whoosh! He had stepped backward off of the cliff. The few seconds he was in freefall to the bottom of the 120-foot hole, he had no time to think or speak. Death had come. Jason was gone.

What happened to Jason would be labeled by most as a 'freak accident'. Most of us will never be close enough to step off a 120' cliff, but death will come to us all the same. Accidents of all kinds happen every day. We never think that something like that will happen to us, but it could. Jason was very comfortable on that cliff. He had repelled there many times before. He did not know that this would be his last day on earth. Was he ready for what eternity held when he was plunged into it in those few seconds? Did he have Death Care?

TYLER

"Hey, Tyler! How are you?" Tyler Gibson looked around to see who had called his name. It was his cousin's wife, Kim.

"Hi. Oh. Fine, I guess. Say, when did you start working here at the bank?" Tyler had come into the bank to cash a check for his boss.

Kim smiled. "I started here about a year ago. Is there something I can help you with?"

Tyler presented the check and said, "My boss asked me to bring this by and get it cashed for him because he has to work late and the bank will be closed when he finally gets off. Can you do that for me?"

Kim took the check, turned it over a couple of times, hesitated, and said, "Well, really, I'm not supposed to. I mean, this check is drawn on a different bank, and neither you nor your boss has an account with us."

Tyler shifted a bit, "Well, what am I gonna tell my boss? I thought our company had an agreement with this bank, or something like that, to cash our payroll checks. At least that was what my boss told me. Could you do it as a favor to me? Please?"

Things had been rough at the job site for Tyler, and he really did not want to disappoint his boss again. He had made several unfortunate mistakes that cost the company money, and he really needed to get on his boss's good side.

Kim chewed her lip for a moment then smiled. "Well, we do have an agreement with this company to cash their payroll checks. And I know that I can trust you, Tyler. I guess I can go ahead and give you the cash. But I need for you to sign the back of it since I'm giving the money to you. Okay?"

Tyler agreed and quickly signed the check. Kim counted the money out to him, and he was on his way. Tyler arrived back at the job site and handed the cash over to his foreman.

His foreman took the money, counted it and grunted. "Well, at least you managed to do *something* right today. You can go ahead and clock out now, Tyler. I'll see you tomorrow at seven, and maybe you will have a better day than you did today."

Tyler nodded and left the office to punch out at the time clock.

Yeah, tomorrow was another day. Hopefully it would be an easier one. He'd only had this job for about a week, and he needed to keep it. Tyler sighed. How many jobs had he been through? Too many. For some reason, he had a hard time keeping a job. He had a knack for always getting caught up in some sort of conflict. He wasn't a confrontational sort of person; he generally tried to shy away from trouble, but somehow, trouble always seemed to find him. He'd never been good in a fight, so he tried to avoid them at all costs, but he still managed to get involved in his fair share of fights as well. He'd resigned himself to the fact that they were unavoidable, at least for him.

Such had been his life. He had a loving mom and a caring dad, but they had split when he was young. Both had remarried to very nice people, and Tyler had had a "normal" twentieth-century childhood. Yet his adolescence and adulthood, so far, had been rough. Why, he simply did not know. He was only twenty-six, and it seemed that that was just the way the cards had been dealt to him.

About a week after he'd taken his boss's check to get it cashed, Tyler got a call from Kim.

"Tyler? I'm sorry, but you need to bring to the bank the five hundred and forty-seven dollars and ninety-five cents that I gave you for your boss's check last week. That check had a stop payment on it, and since you were the last one to sign the check, then you are responsible for returning the funds."

Tyler's mouth went dry, "But, Kim, I don't have that money. I gave it to my boss."

Kim asked in a quite tone, "Um…Tyler, can you come down to the bank? We need to talk to you."

Tyler said he would be there in a few minutes and hung up the phone. He ran his hands through his hair. Oh boy. What kind of trouble had found him now?

At the bank, Kim led Tyler to the customer service officer's conference room. On the table was the check with "stop payment" stamped in bold red lettering across it. Kim returned to her teller window, leaving Tyler with two bank officers who were seated at the head of a long table. They indicated that he should be seated as well.

The long and short of it was that the check had been reported as stolen by his foreman and the company had put a stop pay on the check.

"But I didn't steal that check! My foreman asked me to cash it for him because he was going to be working late and couldn't make it to the bank before closing. Just ask Kim. I told her that the day I brought it in. She gave me the money, and I took it straight to my foreman. I don't have the money, and I bet he doesn't have it anymore either."

Tyler tried to convince the bank officers that they needed to be questioning his foreman, not him. The officers let Tyler know that they didn't care to investigate all of the details. Whatever the situation with his foreman, that was a matter for the two of them to resolve. The bank simply wanted their money back, and he was responsible for returning the funds because he was the one who had signed and received them.

"But I don't have that much money. We're paid weekly and, even though I was paid last week, I don't make nearly as much as my boss does. I have already spent my salary on bills and other things. I'll get paid at the end of this week, but it won't be five hundred and forty-seven dollars and ninety-five cents. And I have obligations to meet, so that even if it were that much, I wouldn't be able to give it to you all at once."

The bank officers allowed that they understood that he had obligations, and that was why they had called him in, to see how they could work out a way for him to return the money.

Tyler was beyond frustrated when he left the bank. He drove straight to his job. He went into the office to confront the foreman. Things didn't go well. Tyler was fired on the grounds that he started a fistfight. He hadn't. The foreman had thrown the first punch at him, and he had only put up his arm to block the blow. Then, at just that moment, who should walk in but his boss's lackey. He backed up the foreman's story that Tyler started the fight, and since the foreman wrote up the report, who was to know differently? Certainly no one would believe Tyler.

Tyler drove home with a feeling of despair creeping in on him. Then he began to get angry at what his foreman had done. He must've called and reported that check stolen the moment Tyler had gotten in his car to drive to the bank! He'd gotten his money *twice*. Now Tyler was getting stuck, and he also had no job. How was he to pay that money back with no job? Tyler groaned to himself. He was going to have to ask his parents for help. It seemed that he continually had to go to them to bail him out of one situation or another. He hated it. That was just how things always were for him. If it wasn't for bad luck, he would have no luck at all. Isn't that how the saying went? That was certainly how things went for Tyler—always, it seemed.

Tyler was a rather quiet sort of fellow. He was nice and likeable but not very outgoing. He had a few friends, but most people didn't take the time to draw him out. He seemed to have a knack for falling in with some pretty rough characters. Tyler had recently become friends with just such a man. His name was Mitch.

Mitch had promised to get Tyler a job working at the machine shop where he was employed. It had been quite a while since he'd been fired by his double-crossing foreman, and he still hadn't found steady work. Not for a lack of trying; that was certain. But so far, he'd not had any luck. Mitch assured Tyler that a position was coming open at the machine shop soon and he could get Tyler on, no problem. It was a position that didn't require Tyler to know machine work because it was entry level and the company would train him. It had the potential to pay pretty good money too. That would be a nice change for Tyler.

Tyler began spending quite a bit of time with Mitch. Tyler was anxious to go to work, so it was worth the investment of time spent being buddies with Mitch if he could get that job at the machine shop.

Mitch was mostly an okay guy, but when he was drunk, he could get mean in a hurry. Tyler usually just left when Mitch started to drink. Tyler didn't want anything to turn into a confrontation. It might ruin his job chances if he and Mitch ever came to blows. Besides, Mitch and his new girlfriend had started messing around some with methamphetamine, and Tyler wanted no part of that either. He had tried it once, but that was it. He had a friend who got a hold of some bad stuff, and it had fried his brain. Now the dude was almost like a walking vegetable. You couldn't even have a conversation with him because all he would have to do is look away, and then when he looked back at you, it was as if he was seeing you for the first time, not at all remembering that you had been there talking to him moments before. And he for sure couldn't remember what you had talked to him about. No, Tyler didn't need any of that junk. Trouble followed him enough as it was.

Wednesday was Mitch's day off, and he called Tyler Tuesday night, asking him if he wanted to come over and hang out, so he had. Mitch, Tyler, and Mitch's girl, Dena, ended up at the club, playing pool. Mitch and Dena had more than their share of beer while they were playing, and when they finally decided to go, Tyler had to drive because he was the only one still partially sober. He drove them all back to Mitch's place. There, Mitch and Dena brought out some meth they had scored while Tyler sacked out on the couch. It was early Wednesday morning when Tyler was awakened by the sound of Mitch and Dena fighting in the next room. Mitch was yelling and smacking Dena around. Tyler thought he heard the sound of furniture breaking. They were both high, and Tyler could tell that Mitch was getting totally out of control.

Tyler went into the bedroom and stepped in between Mitch and Dena. "Mitch, dude, hang on…"

Mitch landed a right hook directly on Tyler's chin that staggered Tyler backward into the hall. He put up his arms to fend off any more blows and tried to say something to Mitch again. Dena was out cold on the floor at that point.

"Dude! Chill out."

Mitch picked up a chair and swung it at Tyler, but Tyler managed to dodge out of the way. "Why are you protecting that witch? Are you messin' around with her, huh? Is that it?" Mitch picked up the leg of a broken chair and came at Tyler again.

"No. No, you're just high, man. You need to come down and cool off." Tyler was backing toward the front door, thinking he might need to make a run for it. He turned his head to get an idea of how close he was to the door, and Mitch took the opportunity to break the chair leg over his head. Tyler fell down, and the lights went out.

The sun on his face brought Tyler around. He felt a throbbing in his head and was suddenly aware that he was no longer in Mitch's house but in a car. When Tyler opened his eyes, he saw that he was in the front seat of Mitch's car with Dena driving and Mitch seated in the back. He didn't know for sure how long he'd been out, but it must have been quite a while, what with the sun shining so bright and high in the sky. They were out in the country, driving down a gravel road.

Tyler found his voice. "Mitch, where are we going?" He turned slowly because of the pain from his head injury and tried to look at Mitch in the backseat.

Mitch smirked at Tyler. "Don't you worry. You are going home, Tyler, permanently."

Tyler's eyes widened at the shotgun Mitch held in his lap.

He looked at Dena, and Mitch barked, "Keep your eyes in front, little man. Just keep your eyes in front. I'm about to teach you a lesson you will never forget."

Tyler felt the cold steel of the shotgun barrel at the back of his skull, but before he could say or do anything, Mitch pulled the trigger and Tyler slumped in the seat.

They dumped his body on the side of a country road. Tyler Gibson was dead.

From 1980 to 2008 there were approximately 184,992 murders that were unsolved.[3] In Tyler's case his murderer paid for his crime with his life. But that doesn't change the fact that Tyler is now dead. Justice is something we all long for. But where is the justice for all of those murders that go unsolved? Is there such a thing as eternal justice? What will eternity hold for someone like Adolf Hitler? There is eternal justice and those who die without Death Care will have to face it, alone.

CHRISTINE

Christine lay wide awake on her best friend's couch, staring up at the ceiling. She just could not get to sleep. There was no use for it. Tomorrow, she would be getting married, and she was so excited. She never thought that she would find a man she could trust, let alone love and marry. Things had always been rough for her. She had never finished school but dropped out for some reason that she couldn't even remember. She had gone to work at the local diner, but her parents hassled her so much about returning to school that when a guy named Todd began hitting on her, she took up with him just to get away from her parents. She moved in with Todd, and from that point on she was kicked around from one bad living arrangement to worse. She reached a place where she didn't trust anyone and had even lost her faith in God. She had been living at her friend Anna's for the past several months because she didn't have any other place to go. Her parents wouldn't allow her to move back home. She was only nineteen and regretted leaving home to move in with Todd, but she couldn't change the past. Boy, Hollywood was good at selling the image of Prince Charming, but he didn't exist in the real world, or so she thought.

Then Rick came into her life. He was different from any man she'd ever known. Christine could not help falling in love with him. She didn't dare hope he would return her feelings. When he told her that he loved her and asked her to marry him, she was speechless. However, she recovered and quickly said yes. Deep down, she had not expected him to go through with it. She had been told many times that she was nobody, so nobody would ever want her. Yet, tomorrow, they would stand in front of the Jefferson County justice of the peace and pledge their love to one another for eternity. She was getting married. Who needs sleep?

I have the rest of my life to sleep, Christine thought. *And I will be sharing it with Rick.*

Another wave of excitement washed over her. Eventually, she did fall asleep, though she didn't know exactly when, and woke at the crack of dawn, ready to conquer the world.

"By the power invested in me, I now pronounce you man and wife. You may kiss the bride!"

Finally, they were man and wife. As Rick kissed her Christine could not hold back the hot tears that slid down her cheeks. Rick gently wiped them away and kissed her again, a long, slow, reassuring kiss. Together, they walked out of the courthouse, got into their new car, and sped off on their honeymoon.

Christine giggled. "Well, now the real fun begins!"

Rick glanced over at her with a hungry look and took her hand. They only had three days for their honeymoon. Rick had two young girls from a previous marriage. His wife had just walked out on them one day. Rick had done a very good job raising the two little girls, ages three and one. They were so sweet! They loved Christine dearly. Together, they would make a perfect family. So they would only get a few days together before having to come and relieve Memaw, Rick's mother, who had taken some precious time off work just to keep the girls for them.

A cruise it was not, but they were thankful all the same. Rick and Christine were looking forward to their weekend together at a hotel in the "big city," as they jokingly referred to it. They lived in Oklahoma, so the closest "big city" was Oklahoma City. Well, they could've driven down to Dallas, but they really didn't want to get that far away from the girls. Rick had only been away from them for a couple of days since their mother had left eleven months before, and he was very anxious about leaving them. So when he told Christine that they would be going to Oklahoma City, she understood. They could have packed a tent and went to the lake for all she cared. It all seemed so surreal to her. She had gained a husband and family all at the same time, and she was happy. She was so very blissfully happy.

Life for Rick and Christine was like something similar to *Leave It to Beaver*. Rick worked and made good money so Christine could stay home if she liked. Christine chose to stay home with the girls for now. She hadn't had a stay-at- home mom when she was little, so it was very important to her that she be there for the girls. And hopefully the girls would soon have a little brother or sister on the way. When they were all well-adjusted, Christine planned to go back to school and get her GED at least. Rick encouraged her that if she wanted to look into taking some college or maybe just some computer classes at the Vo-Tech, he would support and help her. Life was sweet.

Christine relished being a housewife and getting to give the girls, Kinsey and Kayla, all the attention she had so wanted when she was growing up. The girls were soon calling Christine Mommy, and to see them, you would never know that they weren't blood related. It was a perfect fit.

Rick would come home from work for lunch as often as possible. On the days that he couldn't come home to spend lunch with his little family, he would call Christine to see how his girls were doing. Christine loved having a man who showered her with so much loving attention. This particular day, Rick wasn't going to be able to come home for lunch. He'd just ordered take-out with the other guys and pulled out his cell phone to call Christine and let her know. But something was wrong. The phone rang and rang, but no one answered. So Rick tried Christine's cell phone, with the same result. It was strange, and Rick tried not to feel so alarmed. Maybe she had gone to the store and forgotten her cell phone. Rick sat down at a table in the break room to wait for his food. But a niggling thought at the back of his mind bothered him. Something was wrong.

He could just sense it. Rick called again. The phone rang ten times before it was picked up.

"Christine?" Rick spoke into the phone with relief.

But it wasn't Christine who answered him. It was his three-year-old, Kinsey.

"Hi, Daddy! When you come home?"

That was very odd. Christine never let the girls answer the phone.

"Not until later. Kinsey, where is Mommy? I need to talk to Mommy, sweetheart." Rick tried not to let his impatience show in his voice.

"Mommy's taking nap, on the floor. She's been sleep a looooooong time. She don't wake up. I'm hungry. When you come home?" was Kinsey's reply.

Rick was panicked. "I'm coming home right away, honey. Go get Kayla, and you two watch cartoons until Daddy gets home. Okay?"

Kinsey wanted to chat. "Okay. Daddy, you know what I did? I color picture, on wall. I want Mommy to see. She won't wake up. She sleeps all day. Can I go outside?"

Rick spoke more sternly than he intended, "*No!* Do not go outside. Sit still, and Daddy will be home soon. I'm going to hang up now. You need to hang up the phone too, Kinsey. Bye-bye." Rick did hang up and raced to his supervisor's office. "I have a family emergency at home. From what I can get out of my girl, I think my wife has collapsed. I'm going home to check on things."

Rick's supervisor had been eating his own lunch at his computer. He was surprised by Rick's outburst and came to his feet. Rick had already turned and was halfway down the corridor.

"Okay, Rick. Take as much time as you need," his supervisor called after him.

Rick vaguely heard his supervisor. He was out the door and into his truck, his mind racing with worry.

When he arrived at the house, he found his two daughters watching TV in the living room. Kinsey was happy to see her daddy. She jumped up and ran to hug his knees.

"Daddy! You come home!"

Rick bent down and hugged her, glancing around for his wife while he did so.

"Kinsey, where is Mommy?" Kinsey looked down the hall, "She take nap. My room. On the floor."

Rick strode quickly down the hall and turned into his daughter's room. There lay his wife on the floor. She wasn't breathing, and her body was already cold. Rick fumbled for his phone and dialed 911. He was keenly aware that both of his daughters had joined him in the room. For their sakes, he was able to control the wails that were building in his throat, but he could do nothing to stop the tears that began to flow down his cheeks. His voice cracked as he spoke to the 911 operator.

"I need an ambulance. My wife isn't breathing…"

The doctors informed him that his almost twenty-year old, apparently healthy wife had experienced a brain aneurysm[4]. Approximately eight to ten million Americans have been found to have aneurysms . About 40 percent of those who suffer with bleeding from an aneurysm will die within the first month[5]. His wife had been one of them. Death had come. Christine was gone.

There are many silent health conditions that a person can have. Like the lady who had a headache for three days and then died from brain cancer that she didn't know she had, or the mother of two who had an enlarged heart but didn't know it until one night she died in her sleep. We all have a date with death, just like Christine. She was so young. She had a whole beautiful life ahead of her. Did she have Death Care? Only she knows.

KAITLYN

Let me share one more true story. This one does not end in a death. At least, it has not ended that way yet.

Kaitlyn sighed as she sat at the table with her laptop, adding up bills. Even though both she and her husband, Drake, worked, it seemed that they just never could quite get ahead. Every time they were able to put a little back, some unexpected expense always came up. Of course, part of their mounting expenses came from their growing son, Dillon. It was all they could do to keep him in jeans. If he wasn't ripping out the knees, he was growing so fast that he showed three inches of his ankles after only a month of wear. And shoes! Kait rolled her eyes. That was a whole other matter.

Kait glanced at the clock. Drake and Dillon would be home from t-ball soon. Kait knew they would be starved. So she set aside the bills and went to the fridge to see what she could rustle up for dinner.

Kait normally liked to cook, but tonight she was just too drained both physically and mentally. She pulled out some Velveeta cheese. Then she took a can of Rotel and a can of chili from the pantry. Chili cheese dip was always a quick fix that her boys loved. Not exactly the basic four, but it would fill their tummies without having to go to the store.

Once that was done, Kait went to the laundry room to check on the dryer. While in the laundry room, she heard the door slam, announcing the arrival of her two men.

"Hey, Mom! Where are you?" Dillon called.

That boy had a built-in microphone like no one else she knew.

"I'm in the laundry room, Dillon," Kait replied, but before she managed to get the sentence out completely, her son was standing in front of her. What a sight! He was dirty, sweaty, and grinning from ear to ear.

"Guess what!" Dillon said.

"Tell me. What?" replied Kait.

"No, you have to guess, Mom," Dillon said in a teasing tone.

They played that game often. Dillon didn't really want her to guess the right answer. He really wanted to tell her himself, so Kait would try to think of answers that would bring definite no. Then, after a few were tried, Dillon would blurt the correct answer and Kait would act surprised.

So, Kait asked, "You caught a pop fly?"

They didn't have pop flies in youth five t-ball and Kait knew it.

"Nope. Guess again," Dillon said.

"Um…you hit the ball out of the park?"

Dillon shook his head. "No. Try again."

Kait was thinking of a third answer when Dillon exclaimed, "I got to slide into home plate!"

Kait acted surprised. "Wow! That's great! Did the team win?"

Some of the enthusiasm left Dillon's face. "No, we didn't win."

Drake, who had been listening to the exchange between them from the hall, spoke up. "Well, they didn't win, but you had a lot of fun, and none of the boys were sore losers. I was really proud of you kids."

Kait smiled and shooed her boys into the bathroom to wash up for supper. "I'm proud of you too, son. Now, let's see if you can clean enough of that home plate dirt off to eat supper."

Dillon ran for the bathroom, "Yes! I'm starved!"

Kait shook her head. That was just what she had expected.

School was out, so Kait was able to stay home with Dillon. Kait wasn't a teacher, but she did work in the office at Dillon's school. It was very convenient in a way. The only problem was that she didn't bring home a paycheck during June, July, and half of August every year. But Kait enjoyed the time with her son. Soon, he would be six years old. Kait could hardly believe it. Where had the time gone? It just flies by so quickly. Kait did not want to regret not having spent time with him once he was grown. By that time, it would be too late to change anything.

Summer was always a very busy time for Kait's family. There was t-ball and then swim lessons and maybe even summer camp that year. Her mom had already been hinting about Dillon going to church camp with her church that summer, but Kait knew how Drake would feel about that. No go. Drake had grown up in church but had quit going during his first year of college. Kait had been raised, for at least part of her life, in an independent Baptist church. Shortly after they were married, Drake had made it clear that he'd had his fill of church growing up and wanted nothing to do with it now that he was an adult. Drake's family was full of preachers. They came from different denominations but were all of the persuasion that *theirs* was the right one. Drake wanted no part of it.

After the birth of their son, Dillon, Kait thought that Drake's attitude would soften toward church. It did not. She had tried to take Dillon to church on her own, but it would always cause a fight with Drake once he found out about it. He told Kait in very, very clear terms that he'd had religion pushed down his throat all of his life and he was not about to have that happen to his son. When Dillon was older, if he wanted to go to church, that would be entirely up to him.

Kait was exasperated. She truly did believe in God. How could you not? Look at the earth. It was obviously created. Look at the miracle of life. She had carried a child in her womb, felt that new life being formed inside of her. It was so awesome, so amazing. Then the very birth itself was miraculous. How could anyone doubt God's existence?

Drake allowed that he didn't doubt God's existence, but neither would he push one idea of God onto his son over all others. He said that as far as he was concerned, his son could choose to be a Buddhist or Catholic or Muslim or Agnostic or whatever. He would just let Dillon do the choosing.

After a couple of years of trying to persuade him otherwise and every conversation ending in a fight, Kait had given up. So, in the end, none of them went to church. That was not how she had pictured her "perfect" family. But when life gives you lemons, just make lemonade. That's really all that God would expect of you too, isn't it?

However, Kait's conscience told her different. For a while, it really bothered her. But she had managed to stifle it so long that she only felt the guilty twinge of conscience every now and then. In those moments, she would console herself with the thought that, when her time came to die, she would surely have enough time to say, "God, forgive me," or, "God, save me." It took less than a second to say that. Even if something happened fast, she would have at least half a second to utter that short sentence. God was a forgiving and understanding God. He would understand that her actions had been simply to keep peace in her family.

Even as these thoughts ran through her mind, a small voice from somewhere inside would ask, "But what about those things that you know are displeasing to God? Do you do those things just to keep peace? Do you really think God would allow you to sin just to 'keep peace'?" Kait's conscience did still speak to her. It seemed she could never completely get away from it. So, Kait did what she always did when she didn't want to think. She went to the stereo and turned on the radio to her favorite heavy metal rock station with the volume was up loud enough that she could hear it clearly through every room of the house.

Satisfied that she had drowned out the voice of her conscience at last, Kait went on about her daily routine: first breakfast, and then to get Dillon to swim lessons. After that, well, she would think about that later. She shook her head to clear her thoughts. She didn't want to think. Right now, it just wasn't safe to think. A few weeks before school started in the fall, something happened that really shook Kaitlyn up. She had been going to the bank to deposit the money they would need for their next house payment. But Kaitlyn didn't make it to the bank. A truck ran a red light and hit her broadside. Thankfully, it was on the passenger side and Kaitlyn had been the only person in the car. She was a little scraped up and bruised but otherwise fine. Her car, however, was totaled.

Her good friend, Haley, came to check on her shortly after the wreck. Haley had brought her boys, who were also friends with Dillon. They made it into the house before Haley and up the stairs to find Dillon, leaving the two friends alone downstairs.

"Hi! How are you, Kait?" She hugged Kait and then stepped back when she felt Kait grimace.

"Sorry. I didn't mean to hurt you. I'm just so glad to find you in one piece!" Haley smiled, and Kait attempted a smile in return.

"I'm in one piece, but my car isn't. Man, and school is starting in a few weeks too. What on earth am I going to do?"

They sat down in the living room, and after chatting a few minutes, there was a quiet pause.

Then Kait began. "You know, I was thinking I could have died in that wreck if the truck that hit me had been going a little faster. It has made me think. I always thought that whenever my time came and something happened, I would have time to say, 'Jesus, save me!' or whatever. But when that truck plowed into me, I didn't have time to say anything. I would've been dead and never even gotten one word out."

Haley was a Christian and had talked to Kait before about life and death, heaven and hell, but Kait had always changed the subject before. Haley's eyes lit up at the thought that Kait was finally ready to talk about things of eternity.

"Do you mean you want to repent and trust in Christ?" Haley asked.

Kait looked down for a moment and then back at Haley. "No, I'm not saying that. I'm just saying that it all made me think about what you have been telling me all these years. I still don't think I can get saved. I feel like I would have to choose between my family, Drake and Dillon, or God. I just can't do that right now."

Haley looked perplexed. "But surely you realize that God gave Drake and Dillon to you, just as He gives you every breath that you breathe? Every good thing that you have has come from God. He even spared your life in that wreck."

Kait shrugged. "Yeah, but I don't want to lose my family either. You know how Drake feels about church. My 'salvation' would cause a divorce for sure."

Haley replied, "Can't you see that you are loving the gift more than the giver?" She looked Kait in the eyes and realized that she was getting nowhere. "Kait, how would you feel if you had lost your eyesight in that wreck?"

That seemed an odd question, but Kait replied, "I think that would be just about the worse thing to happen, next to becoming a quadriplegic or something."

Haley pressed, "Your eyes are important to you?"

Kait nodded in agreement.

"How much more important should your soul be that looks out of those eyes?"

That was a new thought to Kait.

Their conversation was brought to an abrupt halt by the kids rushing through the living room on their way outside. When the herd of elephants had passed, the conversation took a different turn. They parted some time later, and Kait was left to her thoughts. Kait's life had been spared…for now. But what about tomorrow? One day, death will come. Kaitlyn needs to find Death Care now, while she still has the opportunity. The next time she is in a car wreck she may end up in eternity. She will have no more second chances then. It will be too late.

Watching, Stalking, and Waiting

He's there, someone, somewhere in the shadows.
Lurking, always lurking, there waiting.
Waiting for what?
I turn quickly, but he is gone. I know he was there.
Watching me, waiting, always waiting.

I run, but he follows. I turn, I dart,
I lunge, but still he follows.
I cannot see him, but I know he is there.
I can feel his stare.
His penetrating gaze goes through me.
He terrifies me.
Day and night, he follows, every step,
every breath, every heartbeat.
Oh, how can I escape him?

There is nowhere to hide! He finds me.
He always finds me.
He watches me and waits.
Waiting, but for what?
Who is he? What does he want?

I turn, rage replacing my fear. I yell into the
darkness at the shadowy figure that I cannot see,
"Who are you? What do you want?
What are you waiting for?"
I whirl around, and I am face to face with him.

My heart stops. My body turns cold.
I am face to face with Death.
And, oh, the grin, the awful, hideous grin
on that pale, sunken face!
I try to scream, but find that I cannot.
I try to resist him, but I cannot!
He takes my hand and pulls me into the
blackness that surrounds him.
And just like that, my life is gone.

WHILE WE'RE ALIVE

Reid walked out of the funeral home to sit on the front steps. He watched all of the cars buzzing by. He saw people coming in and out of the restaurant across the street. He thought about the fact that they were totally unaware of his grief. His dad's death had rocked his world, but it did not make life stop for everyone else. Life had ended for his dad, and no one knew it. No one else stopped living their life. He was still alive to live his, although he knew that things would never be the same again. But days, weeks, and months went by, and he found that the world kept on turning. Life did continue, for him. But he would never have his dad back, never hear his voice or see him laugh or hear him play his guitar. He wouldn't be there to share advice and give direction. *Dad will never hold my children,* Reid thought as tears flowed down his cheeks. *Death is so final.*

I am sure you understand. Perhaps you have had an experience like this. Your cell phone rings:

"Hello? Jean? This is Sydney. Did you hear about Ben Smith? He died today. They just didn't catch his colon cancer early enough. It had spread too much. You knew he was undergoing both chemo and radiation, right? Well, he's at peace with God now, rest his soul. I'll let you know when the funeral is. I figure we should take some food by to his family. I will give you more details when I hear. Okay. Catch ya later."

What do you do after a phone call like that? Do you shake your head and say, "Man, he was only a year younger than me! What a shame for someone so young to die like that." You fix food and take it to the family. You send a sympathy card or flowers or both. Perhaps you go by the funeral home and sign the visitation book. Still, your own death seems so far away.

But maybe it's closer than that. Perhaps you have lost a close relative, a husband or wife, mom or dad, brother or sister of your own. They are gone, and it hurts. You cry. You think of how life will never be the same without them. Yet you still have a life. You are not dead. Why? Why wasn't it you? Have you ever asked yourself that? Why is it that some people die young and others die old? We all want to be one of the ones who die old, but we have no guarantee. There is no way to know for certain when any of us will die. And death is no respecter of persons. Why is it then that we never think it will happen to us? Every year, over 2.4 million people die[6], but not us.

Think about it. You will be dead more years than you were alive. The Roman Emperor Constantine lived to be fifty- seven years old, but he's been dead for over 1,500 years. He's still dead today. In the play *Rosencrantz and Guildenstern Are Dead* by Tom Stoppard, the character of Rosencrantz poses a thought-provoking question. He asks, "Eternity's a terrible thought. I mean where's it all going to end?"

What do you think happens after you die? Some people think you go to heaven. Some think that you are reincarnated, sort of like when you play a video game and you die and, "Game Over," flashes across the screen. So what do you do? Start the game again. No big deal. Some think that nothing happens at all when you die. You just simply cease to exist.

I have heard people say, "Well, I'll worry about that when my time comes." Okay. When will that be? As seen in this book, often, you don't have a chance to do anything. Death can come very swiftly. Can you really afford to wait until you are looking death in the face to decide what to believe, to get your life in order? It would be foolish to put it off to the last minute only to find out that, when death comes, you don't even have a minute.

So how do you view this life? How can you know for sure what happens when you die? Some people believe there is a place called hell that would be your destination And it's not a very nice place. I ask you again, how can you know?

Let's play "what-if for a moment. What if there is a heaven and hell? Where would you go? Are you good enough to go to heaven? I am sure that most people would agree that Hitler should have a place reserved for him in hell, but what about the rest of us "ordinary" Janes and

Joes? Well, the Bible gives us the standard for those who can enter heaven and for those who will go to hell. It's the Ten Commandments. "If thou wilt enter into life, keep the commandments" (Matthew 19:17b) Do you think you have kept the Ten Commandments? Let's look and see.

Have you ever told a lie? If you answered yes, well, then that would make you a liar, wouldn't it? And the ninth commandment tells us not to lie. Have you ever stolen anything? (God sees even the small things you've taken.) That would make you a thief. The eighth commandment tells us not to steal. Did you know that Jesus said when we look with lust, we commit adultery in our hearts? Have you ever done that? Honestly, who of us has not? That makes you an adulterer or adulteress in the eyes of God. The seventh commandment tells us to not commit adultery. Have you always loved God with all your heart? Have you loved Him more than you loved yourself and always tried to please Him? None of us have done that, yet the very first commandment tells us we are not to put any god (any person or thing) before Him.

I have just given you four of the Ten Commandments. How did you do? Don't lie now. Did you meet the standard for going to heaven? Would you be guilty of breaking God's laws? If you are honest with yourself, you will admit that you are guilty of being a lawbreaker. We are all guilty of breaking God's law. So if you have broken God's law, are you then worthy of the punishment for your crime, that punishment being eternity in hell? Or does hell sound too harsh to you? Shouldn't the punishment fit the crime? Yes, and it does.

Think about it, if I lied to my nine year old daughter the repercussions of that would be her hurt feelings. If I lied to my husband he would get upset and probably decide he didn't want to take me out to dinner. If I lied to my boss I would probably get fired. If I lied to a judge, well, that's perjury and I might face some jail time or at the very least a pretty steep fine. You will notice, in each of these examples, my crime stayed the same. The only thing that changed was the person I told the lie to and the consequences of telling that lie. As the person's authority increased so did the consequences. With that in mind, realize that when we lie, steal or lust we are violating the laws of our Creator. He has given us everything, our family, our friends, every breath we take. It's all a gift from Him, and yet we think nothing of breaking His laws. We think that He should just smile and sort of shrug it off. Would a judge do that? Would a judge allow perjury in the courtroom to go unpunished? No, a just judge would not. He would see that I was punished and the severity of my punishment would depend on who I'm dealing with. The repercussions vary depending on who my sin is against. The repercussions for lying to my daughter are much less severe than it would be if I lied to say, a judge or the President of the United States.

In that context, think again about the fact that all sin is against God. Every time we lie, steal, lust or blaspheme it is against God. You can't get higher up on the ladder than that. So, Yes, we all deserve hell. But God loved us and did something awesome for us. He sent His only son, Jesus, to die on the cross. Jesus took our punishment. We broke God's law, but Jesus paid our penalty with His own blood!

If you repent of your sins and put your faith in Jesus Christ, you will be saved from hell. You see, God, the holy judge of the universe, can let us go free because Jesus took the just penalty for our sins on himself. Justice has been served in Jesus Christ.

It is so simple! Repentance of sins and faith in Jesus Christ. "Well," you might say, "I'm fine then. I pray every night. I ask God to forgive me all the time so I have it taken care of." No, repentance is not merely admitting you've sinned and saying you're sorry. By definition, it means to "change one's mind"[7]. It is doing what the armed forces call an about-face. You are marching in one direction. Repent! About-face! You are now marching in the opposite direction.

And faith is not merely acknowledging the existence of God. You must have faith and trust in Jesus just like you would trust a lifeboat. The *Titanic* of Life is sinking. You can't just look at the lifeboat and say, with confidence, "I know that lifeboat can save me ." No! You would have to get in the lifeboat. Then you could say, "I'm saved."

Once you have repented of your sins and trusted in Christ as your Savior, you can know that you will go to heaven when you die. That's DeathCare. Now you're covered.

QUESTIONS

Perhaps you are laughing at this. Maybe you are saying, "But I don't believe in God or the Bible." Maybe you are genuinely wondering if you should trust the Bible. How do you know that what the Bible says is true? How can you know that there is a God and that the Bible is His Word? Those are legitimate questions. Let me see if I can give you some good answers.

First, how can we know that there is a God at all? In all cultures throughout all time, people have believed in God or many gods. Why is that? Was it because they simply did not have the scientific "knowledge" and technology that we have today to explain how things got here? Some would say that is exactly it. Science has explained how we got here with the theory of evolution.

But when you look at evolution, it doesn't really answer the big question of how. How did matter get here to start with, you know, back there in the beginning? The First Law of Thermodynamics tells us that matter cannot be created or destroyed. So where did the matter come from that was involved in the Big Bang? Where did the space for the universe come from? Where did the laws (the Law of Gravity, Inertia, etc.) of the universe come from? In light of the necessities of these laws we must ask, "Who is the law giver?" John Wheeler, professor of physics at Princeton University, concerning the laws of nature, states, "Slight variations in physical laws such as gravity or electromagnetism would make life impossible."[8]

If evolution is true and we did evolve, then where and how did our thought process come from? The human body is so complex that we will never know all that there is to know about it. It had to have a designer.

Do you like to play the lottery? Honestly, I don't even care to try. To me, it is simply a tax on poor folks. Have you ever heard of a millionaire who played the lottery? No. He takes his chance with the stock market because, generally, that gives him better odds. But if you do like the lottery or poker or even the gamble of Wall Street, how would you like to have these odds? You have a one in ten to the sixty-seventh power chance of getting your money back and winning. Would you take a gamble with those kinds of odds?

> One chemist has calculated the immense odds against amino acids ever combining to form the necessary proteins by *undirected* means. He estimated the probability to be more than 10 to the 67th to 1 (10^{67}:1) *against* even a *small* protein forming by time and chance, in an ideal

mixture of chemicals, in an ideal atmosphere, and given up to 100 billion years (an age 10 to 20 times greater than the supposed age of the Earth). Mathematicians generally agree that, statistically, any odds beyond 1 in 10 to the 50th ($1:10^{50}$) have a zero probability of ever happening ("and even that gives it the benefit of the doubt!") Mathematician Emil Borel agrees that the laws of probability demonstrate that: *"Events whose probabilities are extremely small never occur."* [9]

Evolution has not been proven. It is just a tax-supported religion. You have to put faith in the theory of evolution, and in my opinion, it takes more faith to believe that nothing created everything than to believe that God created everything.

Sir Arthur Keith said, "Evolution is unproved and unprovable. We believe it only because the only alternative is special creation, and that is unthinkable."[10]

There is an old joke that goes something like this. The devil approaches God. "You did a lousy job with ol' Adam. I could make a better human from nothing." God smiles. "Go ahead." So the devil reaches down and gets a handful of dirt. God stops him. "No. Go get your own dirt. Then try to make a man."

God is eternal, and He created everything from nothing. The Bible tells us, "For the invisible things of him from the creation of the world are clearly seen, being understood by the things that are made, even his eternal power and Godhead; so that they are without excuse" (Romans 1:20). We can look at the awesome intricacies of the world around us and know that there is a Creator God.

On the television series *The Way of the Master*, Ray Comfort gives a very simple illustration. When you look at a building how can you know that there is a builder? The building itself is 100 percent absolute proof that there was a builder[11]. You don't have to meet him to know he exists. You can simply look at his handiwork and know that he exists. It just makes sense.

"But," you say, "I only believe things that I can see or that can be proven scientifically." Well, consider the *Silent Deep*. That's what the ocean was believed to be for many years. When man put his head under the water he heard nothing so he came to the natural conclusion that there wasn't any sound under the water. He made a test, discovered a fact and came to a conclusion. But was it a right conclusion? It seemed very logical. Since he couldn't hear anything then that must mean there is no sound under the sea.

We now know that he made the wrong conclusion. Thanks to the invention of the hydrophone we now know that there is plenty of sound under the sea, man is just not equipped to hear it. The same is true for God. There is another realm, a spiritual realm—God's realm—which we are not equipped to hear and see. You say that you do not believe in God. Maybe you have put

> your head into the spiritual world, so to speak, and because you couldn't see or hear anything you came to the conclusion that there is nothing to it. There is no God. You, just as man did with the ocean, made a test, discovered a fact and came to a conclusion. Was it a right conclusion?
>
> The Bible tells us in 1 Corinthians 2:14, "But the natural man receiveth not the things of the Spirit of God: for they are foolishness unto him: neither can he know them, because they are spiritually discerned."[12]

Okay. So if there is a God who created everything, how do you know which god is the Creator, Allah, Buddha, Christ, Kali? There are many gods worshipped in the world. Which one is the Creator? The Bible tells us that Jesus Christ is the Creator God and that He is the only way of salvation. "But," you object, "can the Bible be trusted? After all, it is comprised of sixty-six books written by about forty different men over a span of about fifteen hundred years. Can it possibly be trustworthy?"

Well, let's look at some facts. Did you know that the Bible contains scientific information that is accurate even though it was written thousands of years before man discovered these truths? Here are a few examples.

> Isaiah 40:22 tells us that the earth is round. At a time when it was believed that

the earth sat on a large animal or a giant (in 1500 bc), the Bible spoke of the earth's free float in space: "He…hangs the earth upon nothing" (Job 26:7). Science didn't discover that the earth hangs upon nothing until 1650 ad.[13]

In Leviticus 15:13, God instructs the Israelites to wash their hands in running water to remove invisible germs. When Ignaz Semmelweis introduced this idea to, during his time, "modern" science, he was scorned and his theory was scoffed. This caused him so much distress that he was eventually institutionalized and ended up dying in an insane asylum[14]. Today we know that the Bible was right.

God told Job in 1500 bc, "Canst thou send the lightnings, that they may go, and say unto thee, Here we *are*?" (Job 38:35). The Bible here is telling Job that lightening can produce sound. The fact that light, magnetism and electricity are related was discovered by James Clerk Maxwell in 1864. "What could be more different than magnetism, electricity, and light? Yet, in the nineteenth century, James Clerk Maxwell showed that these phenomena were simply different manifestations of the same fundamental laws. He described all these, as well as radio waves, radar, and radiant heat, by a unique and elegant system of equations."[15] It was over 3,000 years later that man discovered this scientific truth that was all the while written in the Bible.

We can also see that the Bible is a trustworthy book when you consider the number of detailed prophecies it contains that have been fulfilled to the letter, especially the Messianic prophecies.

> In the book of Daniel, the Bible prophesied the coming of the one and only Jewish Messiah prior to the temple's demise. The Old Testament prophets declared he would be born in Bethlehem (Micah 5:2) to a virgin (Isaiah 7:14), be betrayed for thirty pieces of silver (Zechariah 11:12-13), die by crucifixion (Psalm 22), and be buried in a rich man's tomb (Isaiah 53:9). There was only one person who fits all of the messianic prophecies of the Old Testament who lived before ad 70: Jesus of Nazareth, the Son of Mary.[16]

There are many, many more scientific facts in the Bible and many more detailed prophecies that have been fulfilled to the letter. They are too numerous for me to cover in the scope of this book. However, if you are still not fully convinced and would like to do some research of your own, you will find many good resources listed in the back of this book.

The Bible is a book you can trust. What is more, the Bible offers the only sure way of salvation. No other religion in the world offers the sure hope of salvation. Buddhism does not teach of a Creator. Buddhism has splinter groups but essentially teaches that life and death are a type of illusion. You are stuck in a cycle of reincarnation, death, and suffering, and the only way to break the cycle is to die permanently by entering a permanent state of nonexistence. But how do you reach this state of nonexistence? You have to follow the Noble Eightfold Path to self-perfection. In other words, you have to work hard to be good, and in the end you get to die permanently. No hope of heaven, but no worry with hell. Where is the justice in that?

Hinduism is very diverse. It includes the worship of many gods in many different ways. They also reject the idea of a Creator. When you die, you get to be reincarnated. If you were "bad," you'll come back a frog. If you were "good," you might get to be rich. Again, no hope of salvation from sin. None of us are "good." Even the best of us have broken the laws of the Creator.

Islam teaches that there is a heaven and a hell, but you can't know for certain where you will end up. If you do enough good works for Islam, hopefully you will get to go to heaven, but you cannot know for certain. The only way to ensure you will enter heaven is if you die in jihad. What an inspiring thought.

There are many other religions that go under the name of "Christianity" which teach you have to "do" or perform certain works in order to be saved. I don't know about you, but I am a rather busy person. There are not enough hours in the day for me to do enough good works to earn heaven. I could fill my hours from now until the day I die with good deeds, and I know that it would not even come close to catching up with my sins.

John Adams once said, "Facts are stubborn things; and whatever may be our wishes, our inclinations, or the dictates of our passion, we cannot alter the state of facts and evidence."[17] And it's true. It really doesn't matter what you might think or wish or hope or feel deep in your heart. The fact, the reality is that there is a God who created this world, and we have violated His law. We need to find a way to be acquitted or we are going to have to pay for our crimes.

This is why biblical salvation is so amazing! You can know for certain that when you die, which could happen any minute now, you will go to heaven.

Imagine you have just died and now stand before your Creator. It will not matter what you sincerely believed before your death. All that matters is the reality that you are going to have to give an account for yourself.

The just judge of the universe plays a video of every thought you have ever had, word you have ever spoken, and deed you have ever done. You hang your head, guilty of violating His law, and then you hear Him pass sentence: "I never knew you: depart from me, ye that work iniquity" (Matthew 7:23). You must now accept your just punishment, eternity in hell.

However, you have a choice. That does not have to be the way the story ends for you. If you repent of your sins, putting your faith solely in Jesus Christ for salvation, then when you die and stand before your Creator, who is still just, he will not review a video of all your sins. Instead, the Savior, Jesus Christ, wraps his arms around you and speaks to the just judge of the universe, "This one has no sins to pay for. They came to me in repentance and I have paid for their sins." Then you hear, "Well done…enter thou into the joy of thy lord" (Matthew 25:21b).

Does this whole scenario strike you as harsh? Why would God, who is supposed to be so loving, even think of sending one of his creation to hell? Let me ask you this. When you learned about the Holocaust in your history class, what went through your mind? Do you think the Allies were right to sentence the Nazis to death at the Nuremberg trials? Did it make you sick to see the pictures of the burned bodies, the mass graves, and the ghostly concentration camps? Did it make you angry? Or when terrorists behead someone on live video, do you get sick in your stomach? When you hear of people selling children in sex trafficking rings, does it make you angry? Something inside you cries out for justice, does it not? If we, as mere humans, ache for justice, how much more do you think the Holy Creator wants justice? Should He let murderers and rapists go unpunished? Should He not care?

He does care. God cares about justice. He not only sees every evil deed, but He also knows every evil thought and hears every evil word. He will mete out justice one day. What will be your fate when you stand before this Just and Holy God? Will you receive the death sentence? Or will you received mercy and pardon because one day you realized that you were a sinner in need of a Savior and turned to the Lord, Jesus, in repentance and faith?

YOU, ME, AND GRANDMA

My Grandma was 93 years old when she passed away. The last few years of her life were very lonely, in a sense, as she watched the family and friends which she had grown up with pass away. She buried her firstborn when he was only a few weeks old. Then, one by one, her father and husband died, and then her mother, her siblings, and their spouses as well. Most of her friends have also died. She has a son, a daughter-in-law, three grandchildren, eleven great-grandchildren, and even one great-great grandchild, but she still felt lonely. Having seen so many of the loved ones her own age meet death, she felt like all she was waiting for her own date with death. She did not plan to be facing death so long after her husband, her siblings, and her friends. She did not want to die young, but she reached a place where, it seemed as if death was all there was left for her. Yet, even though so many had already preceded her in death, she was never anxious to die. She would talk of death in one breath as a welcome relief, and in the next, she would be fearful of facing it. We all feel that, do we not? We piously look down in to a casket and say things like, "Well, he's at peace with God now. Rest his soul." But deep down, we are grateful that it is not us in the casket. Being at "peace" sounds good, but not many want to pay the cost for that kind of peace. I'd like to share with you another quick story.

Bob and Jim were the best of friends. They had grown up playing baseball together, and when they were too old to play the game themselves, they enjoyed watching the pros together on TV.

One day, they were reminiscing about those "good ol' days" when Bob asked Jim, "Do you reckon there'll be baseball in heaven?"

Jim thinks for a moment and replies, "I don't know. I guess the only way to find out is when we get there."

A few months later, sadly, Bob died. About a year after Bob's death, Jim was awakened from sleep by the voice of his friend.

He sat up. "What's that? Bob, is that you talking?"

A quiet voice replied, "Yes, it's me, Jim. I just wanted to tell you that I've got good news and bad news."

Jim replied, "Okay. What is it?"

"Well, Jim, the good news is that they do have baseball in heaven. The bad news is you're scheduled to pitch on Wednesday."

What about you? What did you do this morning? You got up, got dressed, and went about your day without giving death a second thought. You assume that when you walk out the door, just as you have thousands of times before, you will walk back through it again in the evening, and the next morning and the next. In reality, you don't know. You might be walking out that door for the very last time. Car accidents kill 115 people every day.[18] That's one approximately every thirteen minutes.[19]

When you lay your head on your pillow at night, you assume that you will wake in the morning. But did you know that every twenty seconds, a person in the United States has a heart attack?[20] More than 2,500 Americans die from heart disease every day.[21]

The English poet Henry Austin Dobson, in *Paradox of Time,* said, "Time goes, you say? Ah no! Alas, time stays, we go." What if today it is your turn to go? Do you think that I am trying to scare you? I am trying to help you think clearly, to consider that you might not have tomorrow. You might only have today.

Let's call it Death Care. Are you covered?

DEATH

Death came to my door one day
I refused to let him in
He looked at my terrified face
And on his, I saw a grin

You think that you can turn me away
You think you can close the door
But no, you can't; you see
You're not in control anymore

As with all mortals, your time has come
Here I am at your door
I will not leave without you
Your life is no more

With that, he took my hand
And I, so weak, allowed
Him to pull me through the door
And into a dark, black shroud

Death came to me, and I could not refuse
It was beyond my power, you see
And one day, he'll come for you
What then? You are no longer free

Then you, as all, will have to stand
And give account for your life
There'll be no more time
To make things right
For, friend, you have died

And when you stand before God's throne
What will you hear Him say?
Enter in, my child, you are redeemed
Or perhaps He'll turn away

Then into the darkness, the darkness of hell
For all eternity
Death one day will come to your door
My friend, are you ready?

BIBLIOGRAPHY

For in-depth research on creation, evolution, world religions, fulfilled biblical prophecies, "errors" in the Bible, etc., use the following resources.

- *Why I Believe* by Dr. D. James Kennedy
- *Scientific Facts in the Bible* by Ray Comfort
- Creation seminar videos at *CreationToday*: www.creationscienceevangelism.com/
- Creation and the Flood: www.answersingenesis.org/get-answers
- Answers on Bible prophecy: www.thebereancall.org/store
- Questions and answers on any of the issues touched on in this book: christiananswers.net
- *In Defense of Faith* by Dave Hunt
- *Evidence that Demands a Verdict* by Josh McDowell

ENDNOTES

1. National Vital Statistics report, Vol. 58, No. 14
2. Statistical estimate from the National Highway Traffic Safety Administration as of 1/10/2012
3. This is according to Scripps Howard News Service calculations based upon homicide estimates provided by the FBI. The rate at which homicides are solved has been declining during the past three decades. Reference timesrecordnews.com 6/12/12
4. emedicine.com Brain Aneurysm Overview article, accessed 1/10/2012
5. emedicine.com Brain Aneurysm Overview article, accessed 1/10/2012
6. Centers for Disease Control, Statistics for America, 2007 tables
7. Miriam Webster Collegiate Dictionary Tenth Edition
8. Reader's Digest September 1986
9. christiananswers.net article "Where Did Life Come From? Is Evolution the Best Scientific Answer?" accessed 1/11/12

10 Creation Science Evangelism Seminar notebook p.4
11 Way of the Master episode 7, "The Beauty of a Broken Spirit—Atheism"
12 Moody Science Video, 'Voice of the Deep' 1956
13 Scientific Facts in the Bible p.11
14 Wikipedia, the free encyclopedia accessed 1/10/12
15 Article by Ann Lamont first published in *Creation* **15** (3):45-47 and reproduced at *creation.com/great-creation-scientists-james-clerk-maxwell*
16 Scientific Facts in the Bible p.41
17 John Adams at the Boston Massacre trial, December 1770
18 car-accidents.com: Get the Facts Crash Statistics, accessed 1/10/12
19 car-accidents.com: Get the Facts Crash Statistics, accessed 1/10/12
20 www.mamashealth.com/Heart_stat.asp accessed 1/19/12
21 www.mamashealth.com/Heart_stat.asp accessed 1/19/12

www.ingramcontent.com/pod-product-compliance
Lightning Source LLC
LaVergne TN
LVHW011731060526
838200LV00051B/3134